THE HITLER WE LOVED & WHY

BY CHRISTOF FRIEDRICH & ERIC THOMSON

Photo credits: TIME, LIFE, NEWSWEEK, NEW YORK TIMES, ATLAS, THE CHICAGO SUN, THE TRIBUNE, DER SPIEGEL, STERN, QUICK, PRAVDA, ISVESTIA, NOVOSTI, TASS, NSNS, IANA, REUTERS, UPI, AP, PDA, CP, NEW CHINA NEWS SERVICE, SOVFOTO and EASTFOTO.

Reprinted November 2004
Liberty Bell Publications
PO Box 890
York, SC 29745
ISBN: 1-59364-023-4

Produced & Published in the United States of America
by
White Power Publications

Box 21, Reedy, W.Va.
25270

ADOLF HITLER

At no time in recorded history has a leader, a wielder of power in human terms, not a popular figurehead or celebrity, had such a closeness to his followers, his entire people, as did Adolf Hitler. It can only be called a love relationship.

What, other than love, can explain the German people's glad welcome of this humble, but thoroughly-dedicated savior from the Eastern Marches? What, other than love, can explain how the people of Greater Germany remained with him in bad times and good, for better or for worse? What, other than love, can explain the fact that those who remember him love him still?

We loved him because he stood for the best that was in us, and as Our Leader, demanded of us our best. It was never Hitler's Germany. It shall always be: Germany's Hitler, the man loved by his people.

This is why we loved him...

We loved him because he loved us and our children...

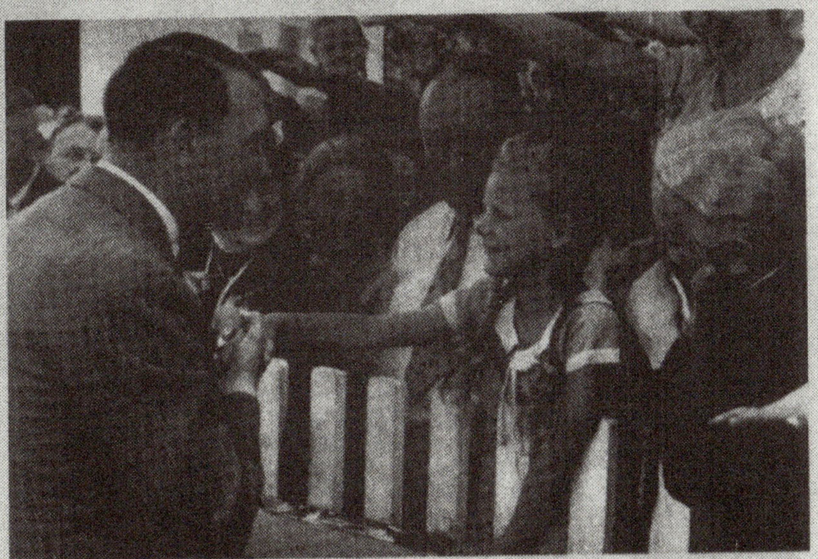

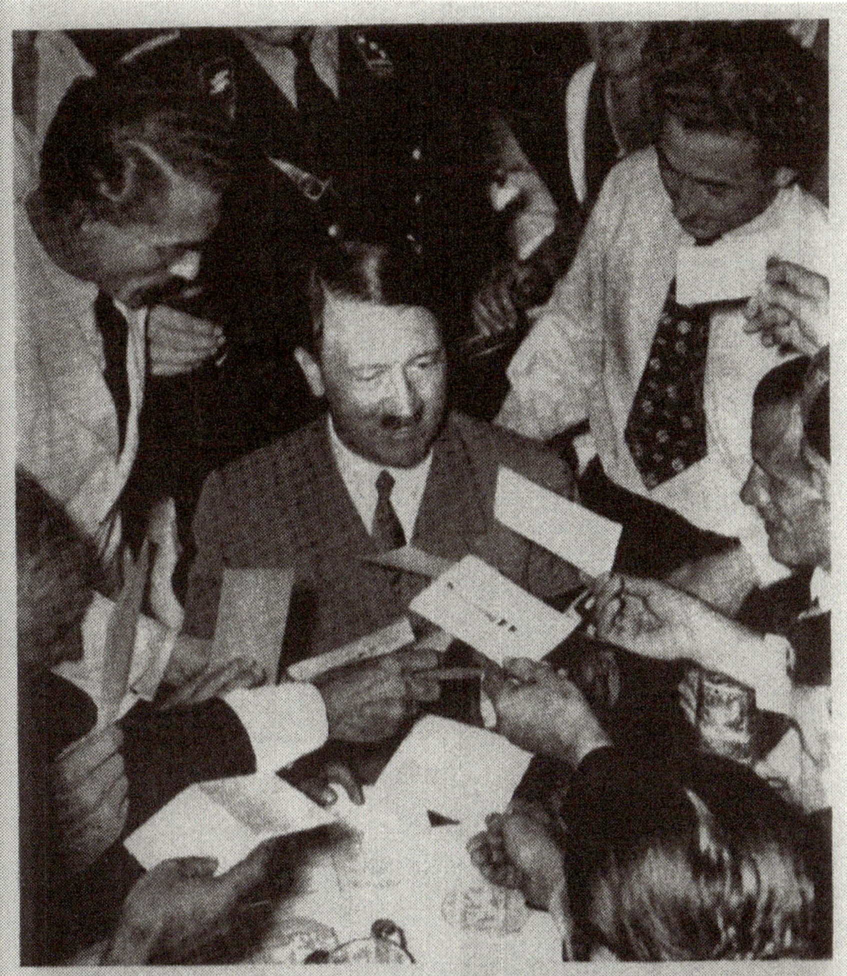

Autographs from the man we loved most. No enemy propaganda can belie this spontaneous show of affection.

A carpet of flowers for the Savior of Germany.

We loved him so much that we, the young and not so young, made pilgrimages to his home in the Alps — not to ask him for favors, but merely to catch a glimpse of him and to be near him.

We loved him because he was a good listener and lived simply.

We loved him because he spoke the unspoken thoughts of our souls in such a way that all could understand. He did not "over-simplify" our problems. He clarified them. He did not beguile us with "cheap" solutions and "easy" panaceas, for there were none. He did not "guarantee" us a better world. He asked us to fight for one. Fight we did, for we who heard him knew he was right.

...Rush ... A Chinese Daily News reporter and photographer witnessed these ... proceedings in a [Japanese] district on Election Day. In a doorway two ... in from the polling place stood a man with what evidently was a registration ... as [each] approached, he would be checked, then sent to a voting booth ...

Returning, he would pause to receive something. Extreme left, a man in a light jacket makes his first stop. Next, a second caller arrives. Third, the secluded camera catches still another caller, as Light Jacket returns. Finally, Light Jacket is back in the doorway, hand extended. The precinct went Democratic nearly 4 to 1.

We loved him because he was honest. He did not expound the supposed virtues of democracy and then corrupt the process with purchased votes. Here, we see democracy in action: 1944 and 1964. The electoral process is no different today.

Democrats Getting Out The Vote

GETTING THE VOTE—It happened in Chicago. At left, a man who identified himself as a Democratic precinct worker, Meyer Mackenberg, gives money from his billfold to a man, center, near the Fifth Precinct.

A CO'IMUNIST POSTER.   A SOCIAL DEMOCRATIC POSTER.

A NAZI POSTER   A NATIONALIST POSTER.

The racial enemy's strategy: Divide and conquer! He tried to
choke our body politic with "choices". Often, we found as
many contending parties as there were candidates. Yet, we were
one people with one choice to make: Whether to live or to die.
We chose life. We chose Adolf Hitler!

"Hard Times" was not just an empty phrase.
It meant empty stomachs...

Empty pockets...

Empty hearths...   Empty lives.

The Jewish bankers' contribution to 20th century art: A madonna and child, portrayed as they die from slow, but inevitable starvation. She was one of many, far too many.

Waiting in eternal queues for a piece of slaughtered dray horse...

The Jewish bankers smashed the economic well-being of the German middleclass. Overnight, massive, bank-created inflation robbed these families of their life-savings, their income of its value. Then, after flooding the country with worthless money, there was no money. Economic life declined from a fever-pitch to the cold inactivity of the grave. With Jewish inflation, the people worked and starved. With Jewish deflation, they simply starved.

Once well-off women of middleclass families are seen selling tin cans, anything to make a few pennies...

Inflation, the worst in history: Not "Made in Germany" — Made in Israel! Germany's banks were owned and controlled by Jews. Although they called themselves the "National Bank of Germany", they were private entities who had appropriated to themselves the right of coining and issuing the money of the German nation, just as they did in England, France and America.

This Jewish banknote ("National Banknote") for one billion marks could purchase approximately one pound of butter in the 1920's.

So much money was necessary for daily expenses that containers became a problem. Those with handcarts were lucky. Billfolds were replaced by picnic hampers, but this was no picnic! A huge basket of money was needed to buy a small loaf of bread.

A crowd outside a Jewish money-changer's shop studies the days rate of inflation. German "pay envelopes" of the Jewish inflationary period: Office workers trudge home with sacks of money. Workers were paid on a daily basis so they could spend their money before rising prices made their wages worthless.

The Jewish pawn-brokers made fortunes from our hardship and battened on our misfortune.

Our enemies have said, "All right, so Hitler gave you order. You Germans are sticklers for order, aren't you? It must have something to do with your toilet training..."

Our reply was this: "Have you ever tried living with constant disorder?"

Robberies, even of the shirts from our backs...

Day after day. Night after night. Year after year!

Disorder: Jew-dominated communists barricade the streets and machinegun law-abiding citizens. The Jews tried to conquer Germany with their Red Terror and civil war, just as they had done so successfully in Russia.

Disorder: Germans turned against one another by alien propaganda battle to the death in German streets.

We were heartsick of disorder. Unanimously, we demanded order!

Hitler gave us order, and he also gave us security and hope.

We loved him, not because he was a "great dictator", but because he was a great teacher, a living example of the order he preached. Without order, nothing can exist. How well we who had suffered knew this lesson!

But when there is no basis for instruction, no racial pattern, no heredity, the lesson of order cannot be learned, no matter how brilliant the instructor. He taught us this all-important truth of race. Hitler's inspiration kindled our racial potential for construction and creativity. His order was not imposed upon us. It came from within.

We loved Hitler because he was a White Man. He practiced our White virtues of forthright honesty and his actions matched his words. If something was filth, he disposed of it as filth with sanitary thoroughness. He did not enshrine the excrescences of sick minds. He was not ashamed to burn shameful enemy propaganda which was aimed at the destruction of our souls.

ANTI-DEFAMATION LEAGUE
130 N. WELLS ST., SUITE 1410
CHICAGO, ILLINOIS
PHONE FRANKLIN 2247

December 13, 1933

TO THE PUBLISHERS OF ANGLO-JEWISH PERIODICALS

Gentlemen:

Scribner & Sons have just published a book by Madison Grant entitled "The Conquest of a Continent." It is extremely antagonistic to Jewish interests. Emphasized throughout is the "Nordic superiority" theory, and the utter negation of any "melting pot" philosophy with regard to America.

Scribners, in a sales circular concerning the book, points to Herr Hitler as the man who has demonstrated the value of "racial purity" in Germany. The author insists that American development depends upon the elimination of unassimilable alien masses in our midst. This book is considered by some as even more destructive than Hitler's "Mein Kampf." Mr. Grant also avers that "national problems are in the end racial problems."

We are interested in stifling the sale of this book. We believe that this can be best accomplished by refusing to be stampeded into giving it publicity. Every review or public criticism of a book of this character brings it to the attention of many who would otherwise know nothing of it. This results in added sales. The less discussion there is concerning it, the more sales resistance will be created.

We therefore appeal to you to refrain from comment on this book, which will undoubtedly be brought to your attention sooner or later. It is our conviction that a general compliance with this request will sound the warning to other publishing houses against engaging in this type of venture.

Sincerely yours,

Richard E. Gutstadt,
Director

REG:EF

He was not like our racial enemy and his democratic stooges who preached freedom of the press and practiced suppression.

Silent Treatment Is Given Book Defending U.S. Racial Majority

CENSORSHIP can take many forms. This is the story of a book that was published but might as well have been suppressed because it has been denied avenues of publicity and distribution to get itself read.

The book is called "The Dispossessed Majority" and it concerns race relations in the United States, recited from the point of view of a member of the white majority. A statement from the publisher about the silent treatment accorded this book concludes:

The censorship of silence imposed by book critics and the book trade on "The Dispossessed Majority" does not prove the abrogation of freedom of thought in this country. After all, the book did get published. But in the final analysis, what good is the freedom to write, if there is very limited freedom to publicize what was written. In order to defend America's largest population group against a continuous stream of often vicious racist propaganda, it would seem that the rights defined in the First Amendment should apply to the dissemination of ideas as well as to their expression.
"The Dispossessed Majority," by Wilmot Robertson . . . is neither obscene nor pornographic. It is a serious discussion of race, amply documented with references to the literature of the field. The author has read widely and writes with apparent familiarity on many aspects of the subject. He covers the concept of race, the racial composition of the United States and a split in the ranks of the majority. Some of the chapters cover the clash in terms of culture, politics, economics, law and foreign policy. While the author's views are controversial they are expressed clearly and logically as a defense of the white Europeans who settled and developed the United States.

The publisher points out that in the last several decades, the ratio of books about American population groups has been 1,000 to one in favor of the minorities and against the majority.

"Two of the more recent and more prominent additions to the bulging pro-minority library," the publisher's statement says, "are the heavily promoted 'The Decline of the Wasp' by Peter Schrag and 'The Rise of the Unmeltable Ethnics' by Michael Novak, which have amounted to little more than book-length slurs against the majority. Several bestsellers by Negro authors have advocated physical vio-
lence against majority members and the destruction of majority property. . . . The intellectual vendetta against the South must be considered a part of this campaign."

The press and the rest of the media have almost totally ignored the book. . . . Libraries and book stores have refused to stock or display [it] and standard publications of the book trade have not listed it. Difficulty was experienced, the publisher says, in placing advertisements. . . .

Among those who speak well of the book is Devin Garrity, a New York book publisher. Rating it as "a major book under any circumstances," he states: "Instead of meekly accepting the assigned role of has-been, Wilmot Robertson, speaking for the majority 'thinks the unthinkable' and says the unsayable,' as one reader puts it. And he does it in superb English prose. . . ."

"The Dispossessed Majority" now has appeared in paperback form (586 pages, including index). It is priced at [$5.00, postpaid] and may be ordered by mail from Howard Allen Enterprises, Inc., Box 76, Cape Canaveral, Fla., 32920.

T. R. WARING
Editor

Editorial reprinted by permission of the Charleston News & Courier

We loved him because he replaced the wasteful idleness of our penal system with productive labor and punishment with redemption. Even habitual criminals fulfilled useful roles in our society, roles which even they could look upon with pride. Not only did he save us from them, he saved them for us.

We loved him because he protected us from religious charlatans — preachers for profit who posed as prophets of God in order to batten like vampires on the trust of simple believers.

We loved him because he defended us against the racial enemy's campaign to spread perversion among us. He knew that sexual perversion was poison and that enough of it could kill any race. Here, the Party newspaper attacks a homosexual Jew who lectured high school students on the "unfairness" of our laws against sex perversion.

We thanked him for removing from circulation the many Jew smut publications which championed all manner of sexual deviation, including abortion, in the name of "freedom of the press".

We loved him because he removed our alien dominators and placed them back among their own kind.

Smiling faces in the Warsaw Ghetto. Jews were happy to be back among their own kind and to live according to their own laws.

We loved him because he freed us from those corrupted by gold
and replaced them with able and incorruptible men.

Incorruptible men: The District Leaders of the NSDAP.

Die
Gauleiter
Vorkämpfer der
NSDAP. und
Schildhalter
des Führers
in den Gauen
Des Reiches.

Da freut sich Gruppenführer Heydrich

Standartenführer Berndt kann auch nicht
klagen . . .

. . . und Oberführer Roesener läßt niemand
„ungeschoren"

We loved him because he did not surround himself with persons who sought idle privilege, but who sought instead the privilege of serving us. No means of helping our people was too humble for our "high and mighty" leaders. We contributed freely, for we loved our leaders almost as much as we did Our Leader.

We loved him because he made our police force work for us, not against us. Our young learned that our police were not a hindrance, but a necessary help in the establishment of a healthy society. Certainly, all available help was necessary to protect the honest citizen from the machinations of traitors, secret societies and minority pressure groups.

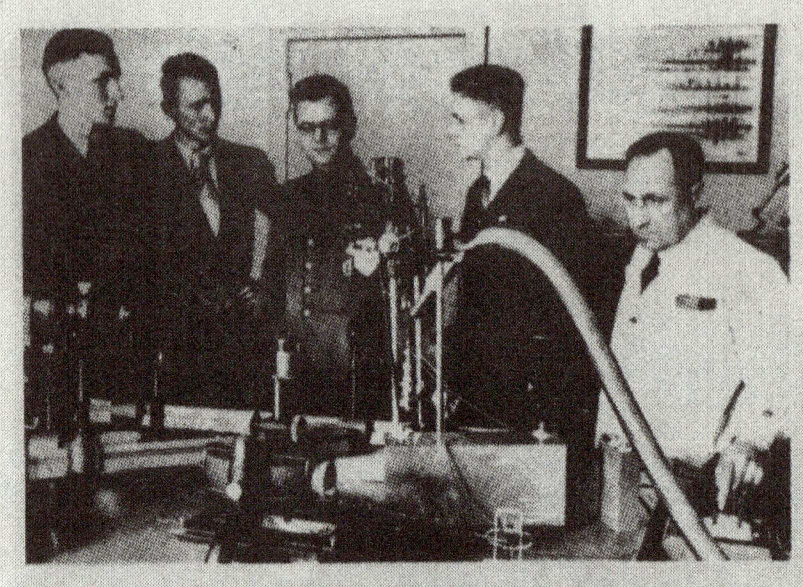

Once again, we supported our police. Once again, they were German police, working for a German government. Thus, we required far fewer police to "maintain public order" under Hitler than we do today, under alien domination.

We loved him because he did not persecute our enemies, but prosecuted them, without fear or favor, according to law — our law.

4 Jews Get 'Life' In Treason Trials

Today's headlines show what we faced, until our Hitler came along.

GOLDREICH

GOLDBERG

BERNSTEIN

WOLPE

COMMUNIST PARTY MEETS IN JEW CENTERS

"There'll be joy in Yablon Cultural Center," exulted the Communist paper, PEOPLE'S WORLD (see inset above) . . . (when) Smith Act defendants, their attorneys and friends will celebrate the recent Supreme Court ruling which freed five and ordered new trials for the remaining nine." So began a recent item in the Communist Party's official Pacific coast organ in announcing a July 3rd celebration in honor of the 14 west coast Communist leaders whose Smith Act sentences were recently upset by Supreme Court decision.

It was fitting that the Communists should hold their "victory" celebration at the Jewish "Misha Yablon Cultural Center" in the heart of Hollywood, because practically all the 14 red leaders are either Jews or (in a few cases) married to Jews. The Communist Party frequently holds rallies, social events and fund raising affairs at various Jewish "cultural centers" in the Los Angeles area . . .

6 Men Charged With Arson in Business Fires

Chief Magistrate John P. Walsh held six men without bail Friday in connection with a suspected arson ring.

The men and charges are:

Stanley Feinstein, 47, of Dorcas st. near Tyson, and his brother, Irvin, 44, of Brighton st. near Pennway ave., arson and conspiracy.

Edward M. Gornish, 48, of 59th st. near Malvern ave., arson, conspiracy and burning with intent to defraud.

Nathan Cautin, 50, of Bluejay rd., Roslyn, arson, conspiracy and burning with intent to defraud.

Edward Klayman, 37, of 57th st. near Diamond, arson and conspiracy.

Solomon Green, 33, of Walnut st. near 39th, arson and conspiracy.

Police said the Feinsteins operate Jack Feinstein and Co., insurance adjusters; Gornish is a real estate dealer, and Cautin is a restaurant owner.

They were held in connection with fires in a restaurant in 1963, an apartment in 1962 and a taproom in 1964.

Bounty-hunter Wiesenthal.

Hatemonger Norden.

These were not Germans, yet, they lived in our midst and worked unceasingly to destroy us!

The Face Of The Enemy

INTEGRATION LEADER RECEIVES AWARD
. . . Rabbi Jacob Rothschild presents bowl to King

We loved him because he saved us from the alien invaders who promoted the extinction of our race, the White Race.

Stars Encourage Mongrelization

Adam West, Ngarua Frisbie

Barb, Doug McClure

Neile and Steve McQueen

Kamala and Chuck Connors

Ron Randell, Laya Raki

By Marrying Asiatics

We loved him because he kept our entertainment media free of the perversion of race-mixing and race-suicide.

Mixed schoolrooms lead to mixed families.

INTER-RACIAL PLAY

LEADS TO
INTER-RACIAL MARRIAGE

CHUBBY CHECKERS NEW WIFE

Singer Danny Williams and white wife, actress Bobbi Carole.

FILTHY JEW MOVIES

White Women And Negro Man

BRAINWASH YOUTHS

We loved him because he used the entertainment media to educate us about life and true values. The themes were uplifting in ways which were never dull. Best of all, they were OUR plays and films, made by OUR people.

Hier wird der Unterschied zwischen nordischem Führertum und asiatischer Prunkherrschaft deutlich. Kraftvoll, entschlossen die Haltung Alexanders, die Waffe in der Hand, Vorderster im Kampf.

RASSENCHAOS IN DER ANTIKE

Nordische Edelgestalten, Schöpfer der antiken Kultur . . . daneben die fremden Gesichter Asiens und Afrikas. Alle aber waren Staatsbürger der antiken Reiche! Norden, Süden und Osten prallten im Mittelmeerbecken aufeinander. Solange der Norde sich rein hält, vollzieht sich großartiger Aufbau. Durch Bastardierung zerfällt die Kultur in Trümmer.

Aufnahmen: Staedtner (12), Deutscher Kunstverlag (3), Buchholz (1)

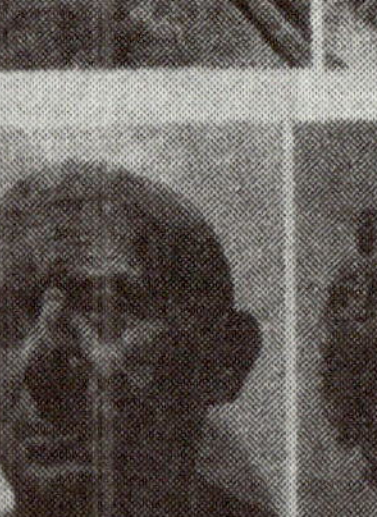

We loved him because he taught us the truth about race and proved, even to skeptics, that the White Race is the founder of all great cultures and civilizations and that race-mixing is the great destroyer.

Flehend, mit angstverzerrten Zügen ohne Waffen hinter der Schar der Leibwächter, auf seinem Prunkwagen der hilflose Darius, Beherrscher des orientalischen Asiens. Kein Widerstand, keine Haltung, nur Rettung von Leib und Leben.

Pictures show the German army's discovery of bolshevik blood-cellars in which innocent civilians of German descent were tortured and finally murdered in Jew-dominated Poland.

We loved him because he hid nothing from us. He was confident in our strength to face the worst atrocities our enemies had to offer — and surmount them with courage and determination.

We loved him because he taught our fellow White men, the Poles, the truth about their Jewish-Soviet "liberators". He showed the world the ghastly face of communism by revealing the Katyn Forest Massacre of the Polish officer corps and by proving forever the guilt of the Soviet system.

We loved him because he had bold plans which benefitted man
and harmonized with Nature.

Here is an artist's impression of his idea for a trans-Alpine ship
canal.

Model of the Nurnberg Congress Hall which he designed to accommodate over 50,000 persons.

Congress Hall's interior.

We loved him because he gave us the best roads in the world, envied and emulated by other peoples ever since. Not only roads did he give us, but a cheap, practical car to run on them: The Volkswagen, the People's Car.

Thank you for giving us honest money and thereby saving our jobs, our homes and our industry. Thank you for making our lives not only bearable, but fruitful.

We loved him because he did the Work of the Lord, by driving the money-changers out of our country.

Thank you, Adolf Hitler, for teaching us that true wealth is not based on gold nor upon credit, but upon the productivity of our land and our people. Honest money is only possible with honest men. No system of law or gold can protect us from criminals in government. There is no substitute for honest men.

We loved him because he wrested the creation of our money away from the Jews, like his American predecessor, Abraham Lincoln. He restored our economy to peacetime prosperity. It was not preparation for war that ended our depression. It was Adolf Hitler. Where the Jews retained their money power, the depression worsened. Unemployment rose drastically in America and Britain at this time. As the British military strategist, Liddell Hart, maintained: The last thing Hitler wanted was war. But war came at last, and none too soon for the Jewish bankers! War was declared by Britain in 1939, but little fighting occurred. Britain announced Jewish terms for ending the war: Kill Hitler and return to the international gold standard. For Germany, the choice was certain death by starvation or possible death in battle.

The Jewish bankers had created massive unemployment in our country, just as they had done in England, France, America and throughout the world. They did this by decreasing the supply of money, which our racial renegade governments had allowed them to control entirely.

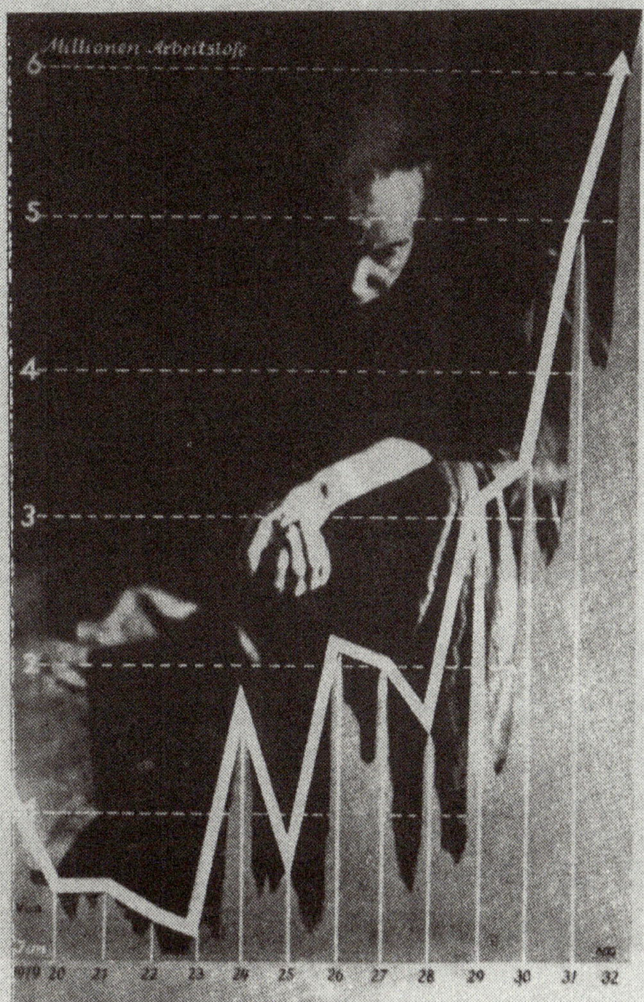

Before Hitler came, over seven million Germans were unemployed and over six million only partially-employed. In the four bleak years from 1929 to 1933, despair and hopelessness caused the death by suicide of some 250,000 of our people.

In four years, from 1933 to 1937, he made us virtually self-sufficient in our domestic requirements of...

Steel...

Aluminum...

5 000 000 000 RM
Salzsäure
rein
Ammoniak
rein
Ammoniak
rein
2 800 000 000 RM
1933
1934
1935
1937

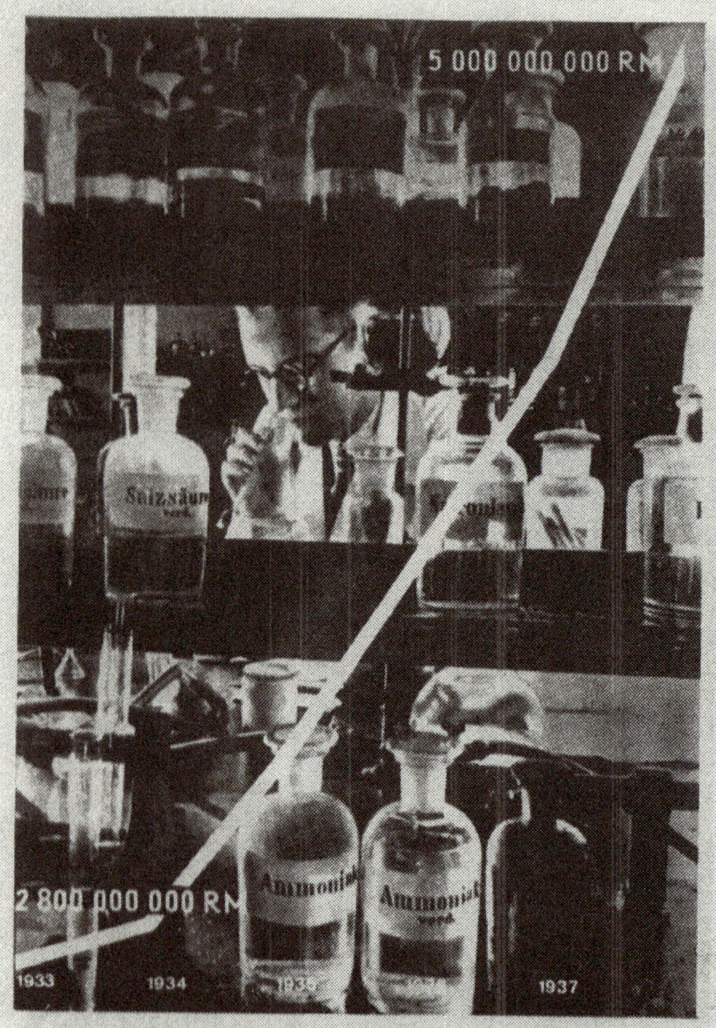

Chemicals...

Petroleum

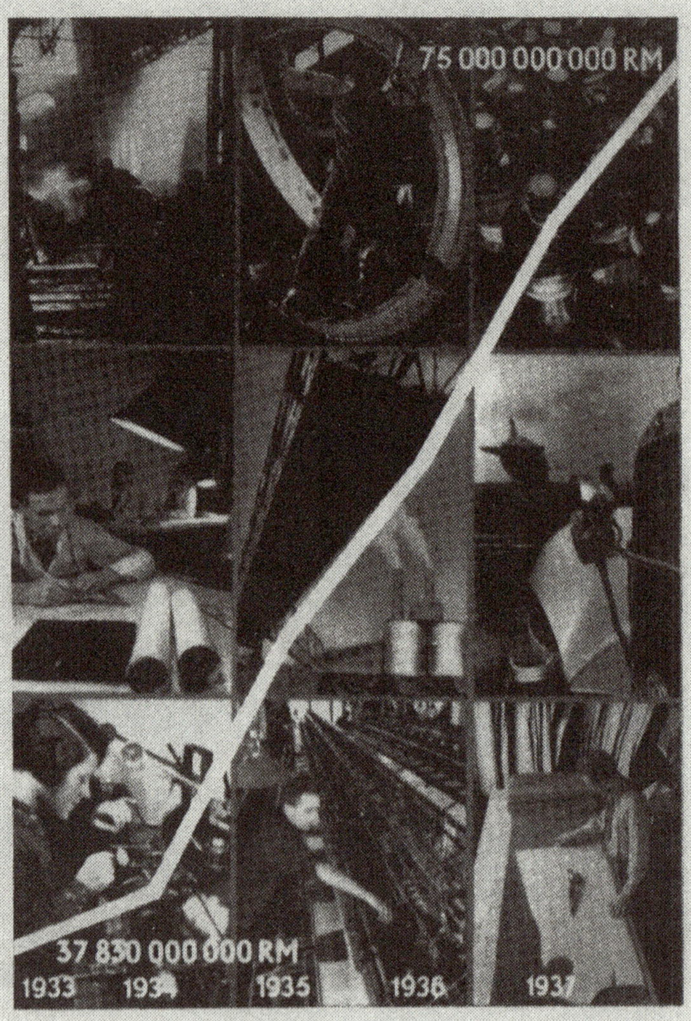

General industrial production...

We loved him because he freed us from dire dependency on the whims and vagaries of foreign suppliers of domestic necessities. He taught us that political independence was possible only with economic independence.

We loved him because he had deep reverence for our past. A people whose roots are strong cannot be toppled by gusts of fad, fashion and foolish innovation.

Our leaders are seen making a solemn pilgrimage to The Dome, site of repose for the remains of our ancient kings.

We loved him because he was a deeply spiritual man who did
not allow Jews to confuse Christian teachings.

The Christian churches loved him. Over 40% of the SS were Catholics.

We loved him because he built churches for us, Christian churches. In the name of Christianity, our enemies destroyed these churches, later bragging about the "precision" of their bombing raids.

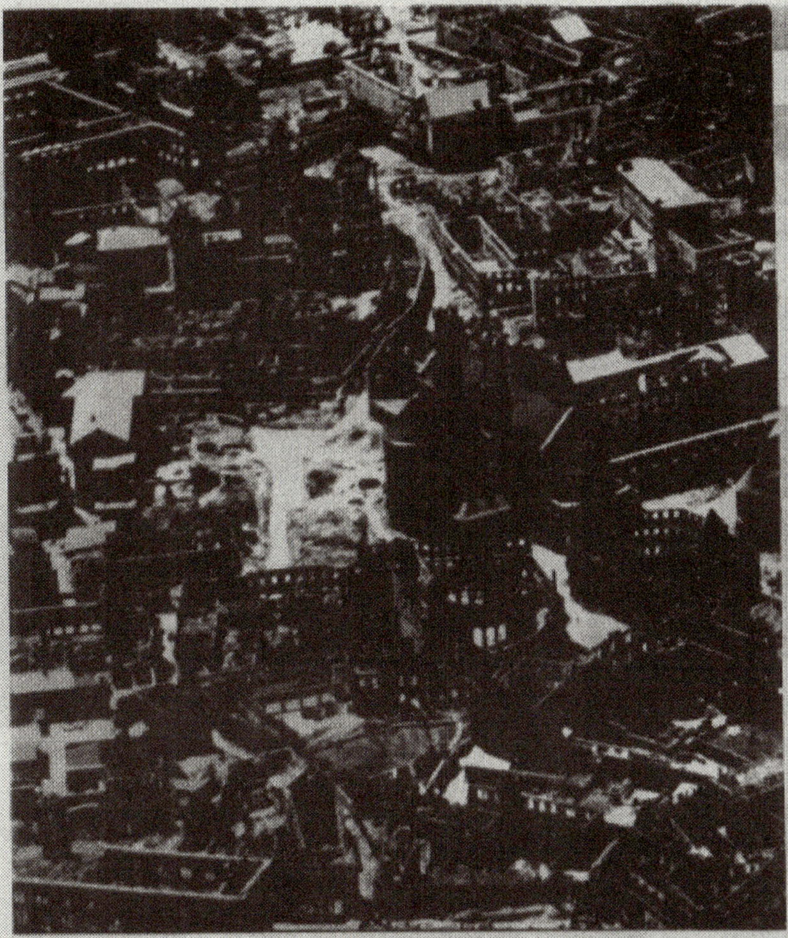

Today, rabbis lecture in "Christian" schools. The Talmud of the Jews has not changed. This is their "holy of holies" which describes non-Jews as "beasts of the field", "cattle". The Jews have not changed. Why have the Christians changed?

We loved him because he loved his parents. Hitler meditates at
the side of his parents' grave.

We loved him because he loved and respected our fellow White nationalists who understood the necessity for White Solidarity.

Charles Lindbergh and his wife are entertained by Reichsmarschall Goering.

The Duke and Duchess of Windsor visit Hitler.

We loved him because he reaffirmed the goodness and the wisdom of wholesome work and wholesome food.

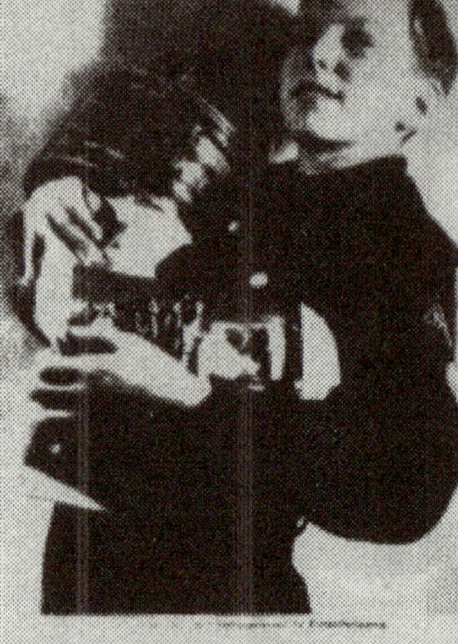

Kampf dem Verderb!

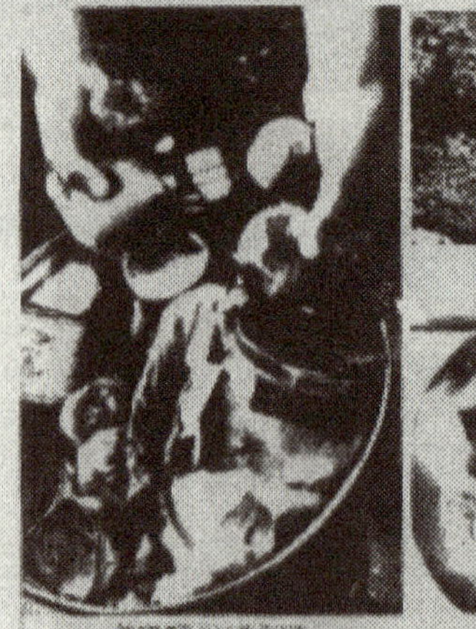

We loved him because he taught us the importance of good food, its proper storage and its relationship to good health. The use of chemical food additives and food substitutes was discouraged. Nutrition came before profit; quality before quantity.

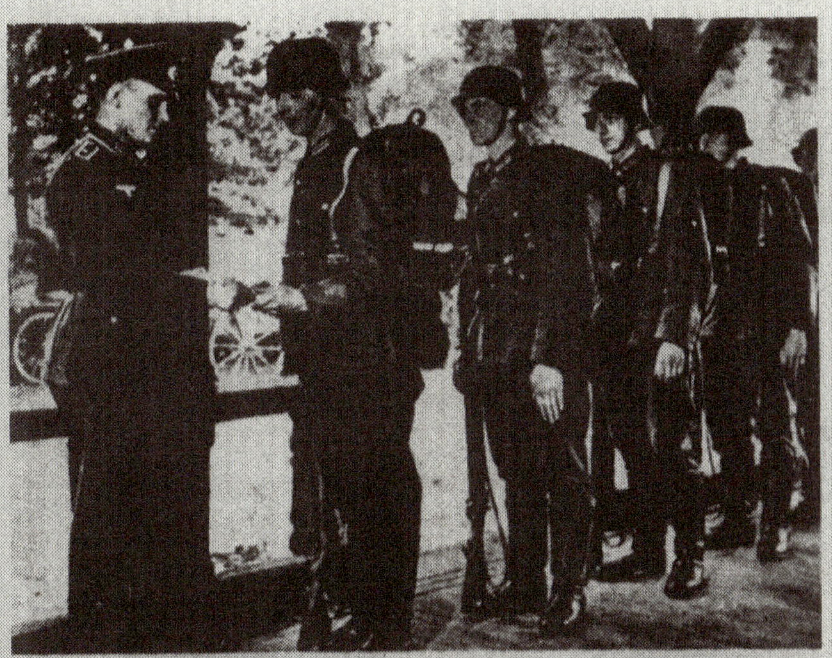

Soldiers receive daily rations of Vitamin C.

We loved him because he loved our fellow-creatures.

Man's best friend was not forgotten, even in wartime. Here, we
see ration cards for dogs.

We loved him because he joined us in our holy festivities:
Christmas, 1938.

Ad for Mauser hunting rifles taken from a 1938 edition of the German magazine, "Work & Leisure".

We loved him because he trusted us. No true Leader need fear the armed members of his own race.

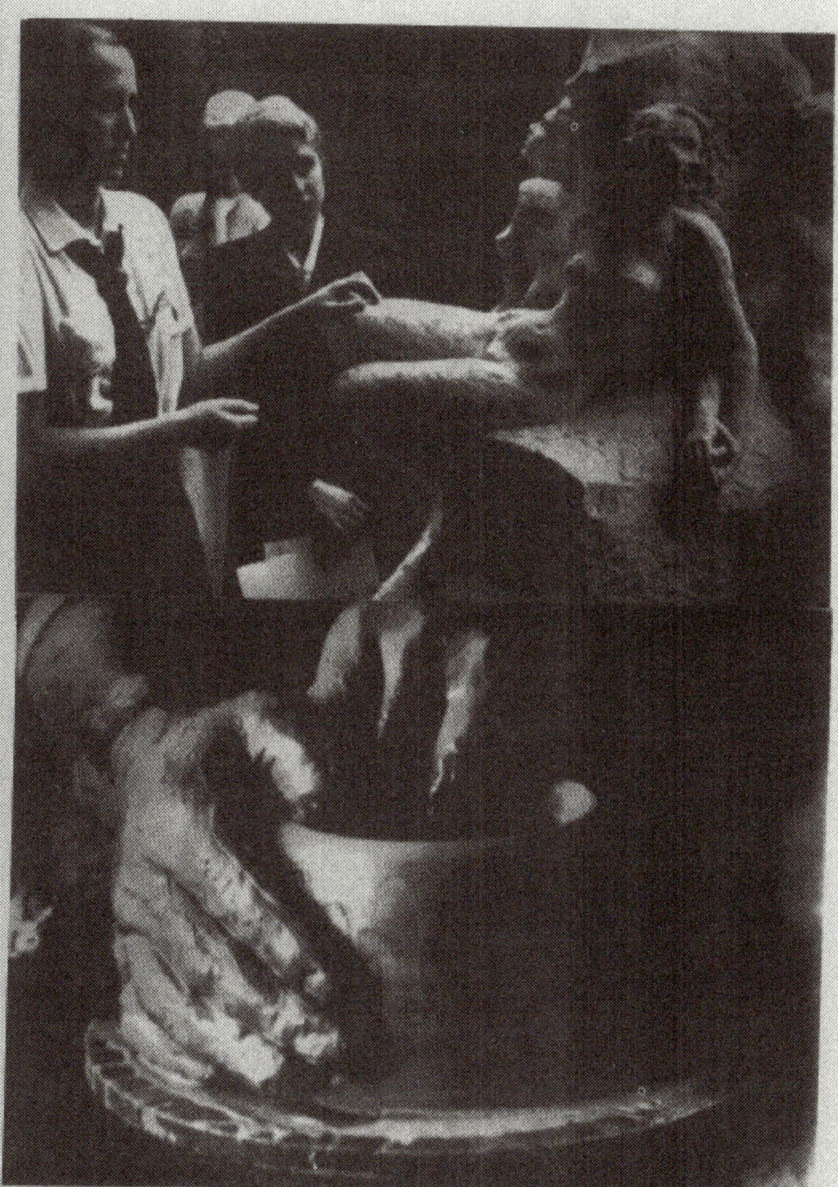

We loved him because he taught us to appreciate beauty by creating it with our own hands. Perfection and excellence were our goals. As we worked to master our medium, we learned to observe Nature and to apply Her Laws. Thus did we become artists and also, National Socialists, for National Socialism is simply the application of Nature's Laws to politics.

We loved him because he encouraged the sexes to realize their full potentials, as complementary rather than competitive beings. Men were made for women and women for men. Each was trained for that which he or she could do best. This did not mean that men could not be artistic or creative, nor did it mean that women could not be great aviatrixes, photographers, film-directors, athletes, etc. It simply meant that, whatever we did, our men were manly and our women feminine. Enemy inculcation of sexual role-confusion with the aim of crippling the sexes' role in child-rearing was thus overthrown and scattered to the winds.

Here, we see women designing their own clothing, clothing which graced their healthy figures, clothing which appealed to men. How unlike today, wherein persons of dubious sexual identity design garments for masochists of both sexes which children would recognize immediately as circus clown costumes, not "fashion".

We loved him because he devoted much effort and care to provide the unborn and parents-to-be with a healthy and pleasant environment.

Beginning with healthy young parents, Hitler encouraged good prenatal care by stressing healthy diet, exercise and freedom from intoxicants.

A Hitler youth helps a policeman check a young man's identification. Smoking and drinking were forbidden those under eighteen years of age.

The unhealthy and the mentally-defective were discouraged from inflicting more of themselves upon our hard-pressed population.

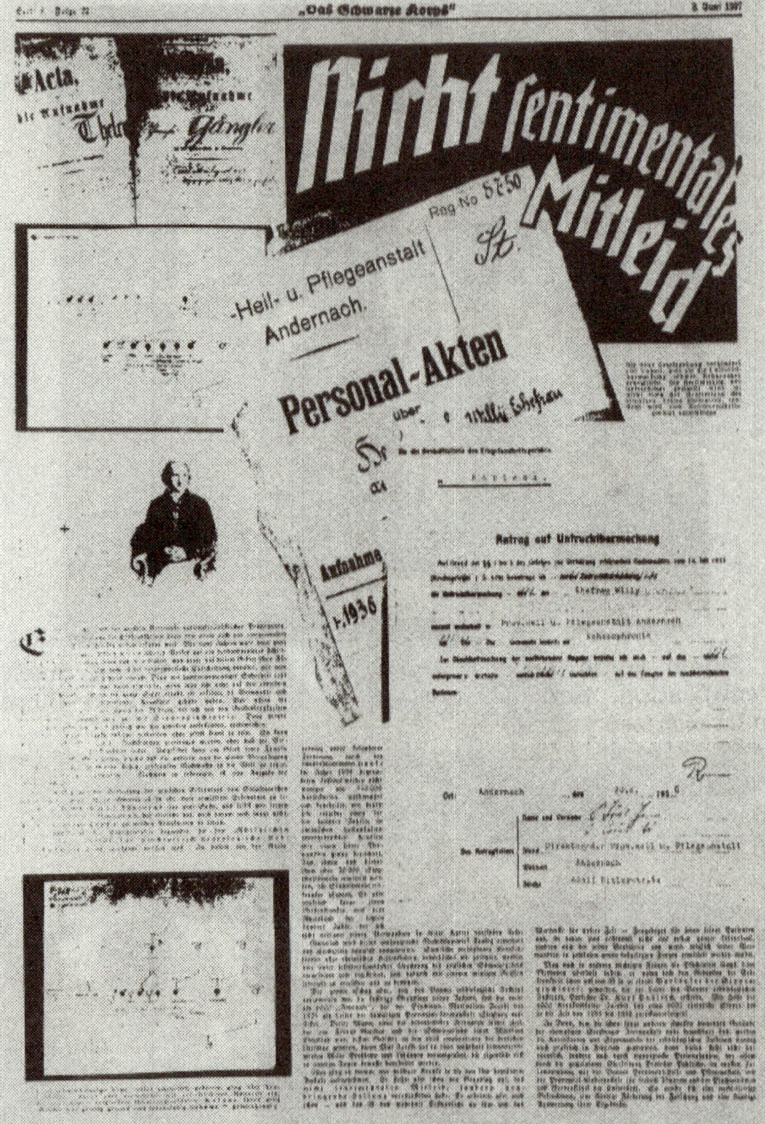

Sterilization was recommended for carriers of severe genetic defects. Here, we see medical certificates of fitness or unfitness for child- bearing. The German people could decide who should have children — not the Jewish bankers.

The healthy and the mentally-fit were encouraged to have large families.

Mozart, 7th of 7 children.

Bismarck, 4th of 6 children.

Philosopher, Immanuel Kant,
4th of 9 children.

Fieldmarshall von Bluecher,
7th of 7 children.

Large families have never been responsible for imbecility, not when the parents were normal, healthy men and women, as these pictures show. Even less so were idiots, morons and imbeciles possible under National Socialism, simply because such sorry specimens were not allowed to reproduce. Large families increased the certainty of geniuses, thus defeating the random probability curve of the genetic defeatists.

Hitler taught us Nature's Way of preserving our race by having large families. Thus, Nature could help us in the fulfillment of our racial destiny by selecting of us our best.

Johann Sebastian Bach,
6th of 12 children.

Frederick the Great,
4th of 14 children.

Richard Wagner,
9th of 9 children.

General Ludendorff,
3rd of 6 children.

So-called experts on human genetics claim today that man is not part of Nature when it comes to heredity! Healthy animals can mate, but healthy humans are something else entirely. These "experts" claim that human health is too difficult to define for purposes of child-bearing, as if mankind has suddenly lost all medical knowledge and can no longer distinguish cripples from accomplished athletes and idiots from geniuses.

Here is shown a typical home for unwed mothers.

We loved him because he loved life and protected the rights of the unborn.

Motherhood was not a crime! We loved him because he provided the best facilities for mothers-to-be. Healthy children were precious — all of them — whether born in or out of wedlock. Unwed mothers also deserved our love, as they do today. Babies were not disposable, like plastic containers. Nor were they seen as intolerable inconveniences. Hitler, the artist and designer, designed a society for loving human beings, not plastic dummies.

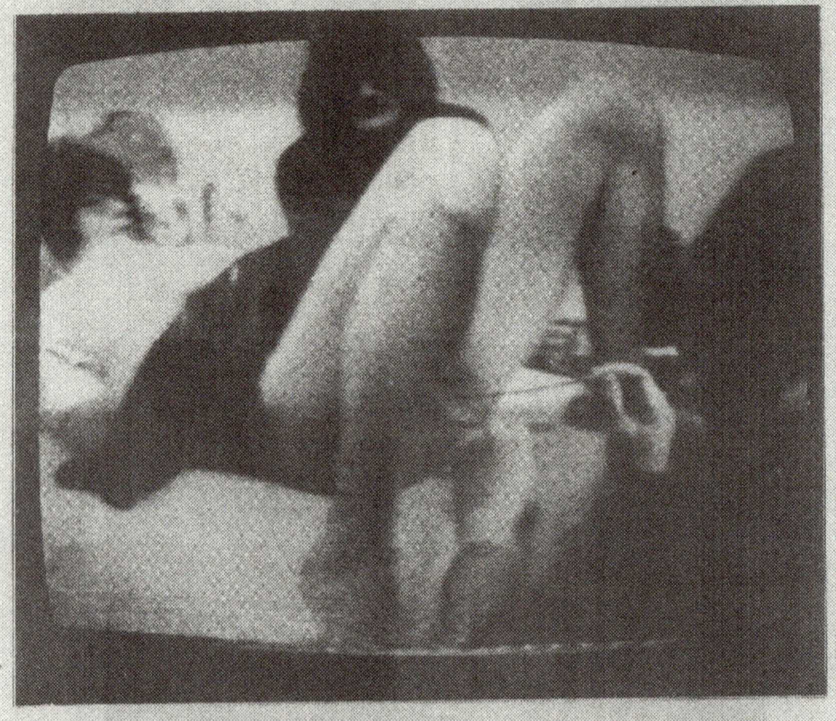

Today: An alien system televises the murder of the unborn. Could Rome, at the nadir of its decadence, surpass this?

If we are sufficiently educated so that we are not confused by the fallacious arguments of the anti-eugenicists, then we are asked, "Who can be trusted to decide who is or is not fit to have children?"

Hitler's answer was blunt: "Until now, Jewish bankers have decided. From now on, the German people will decide!"

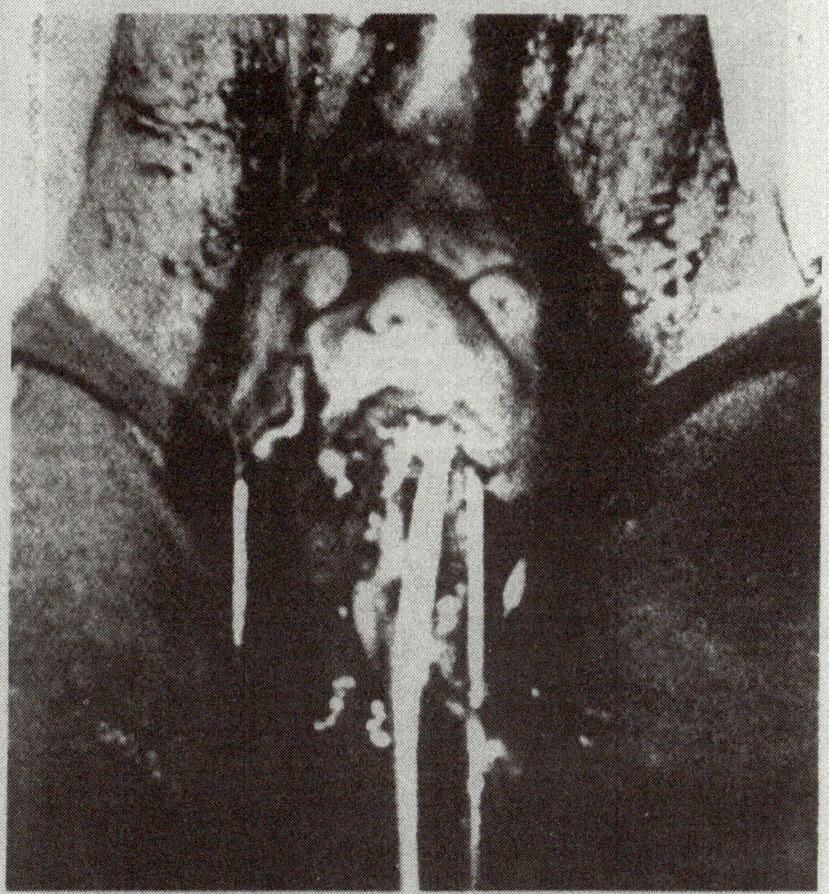

A child is torn to pieces by abortion surgery. Shown is a close up view of the murdered infant's head, trailing fragments of its shattered body. Were any of the previously-noted great men of art, music or statesmanship conceived today, they might have perished because they were viewed as "too expensive" or "too inconvenient" for either or both of its parents. It is certain that none of the geniuses depicted in the previous pages would have survived in the present day two-child families.

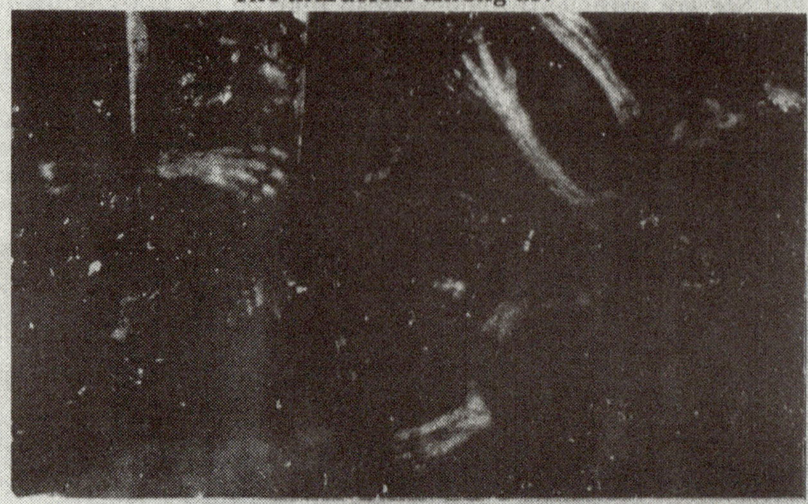

Suction Abortion at 10 Weeks

Over 75% of all abortions performed in the U.S. and Canada are done by this method. It is like the D & C except that a powerful suction tube is inserted. This tears apart the body of the developing baby and his placenta, sucking the "products of pregnancy" into a jar. Sometimes the smaller body parts are recognizable as on this picture.

Caesarean Section Abortion (Hysterotomy)

The baby in this picture weighing two pounds (a 24 week pregnancy) was to be aborted. She was cut free, dropped in a bucket, and left to die. At this age they all move, breathe and some will even cry.

In 1971, about 4000 of these abortions were done in New York. Since all of these babies are born alive, this means that 4000 babies were aborted alive and left to, or encouraged to, die.

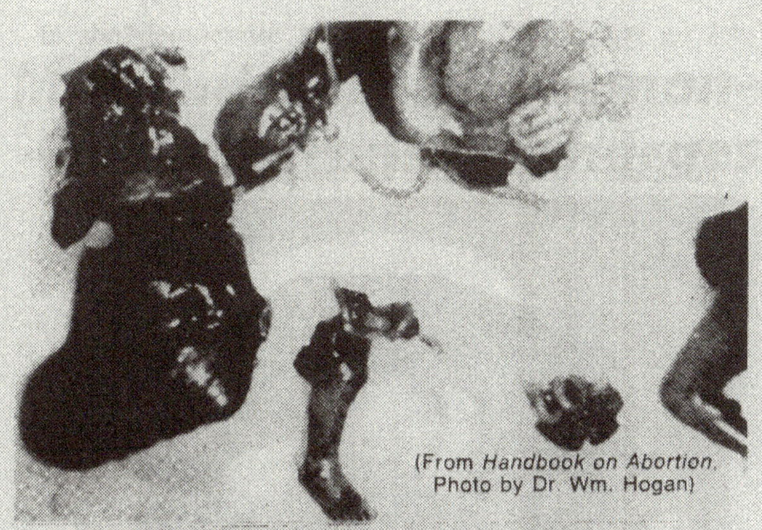

D & C Abortion at 12 Weeks

Performed between 7 and 12 weeks, this method utilizes a sharp curved knife. The uterus is approached through the vagina. The cervix (mouth of the womb) is stretched open. The surgeon then cuts the tiny body to pieces and cuts and scrapes the placenta from the inside walls of the uterus. Bleeding is usually profuse.

One of the jobs of the operating nurse is to reassemble the parts to be sure the uterus is empty, otherwise she will bleed or become infected.

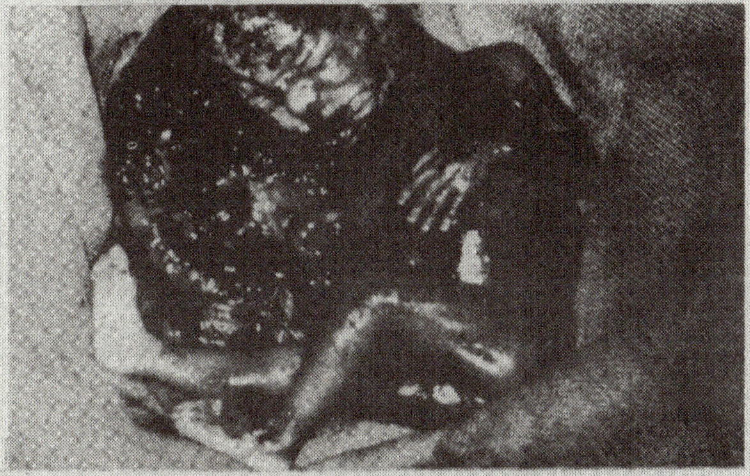

Salt Poisoning Abortion at 19 Weeks

This method is done after 16 weeks when enough fluid has accumulated in the sac around the baby. A long needle is inserted through the mother's abdomen into the baby's sac and a solution of concentrated salt is injected into it. The baby breathes in and swallows the salt and is poisoned by it. The outer layer of skin is burned off by its corrosive effect. It takes over an hour to slowly kill a baby by this method.

Our racial enemy and his dupes dare accuse us of bogus atrocities! They commit the real ones.

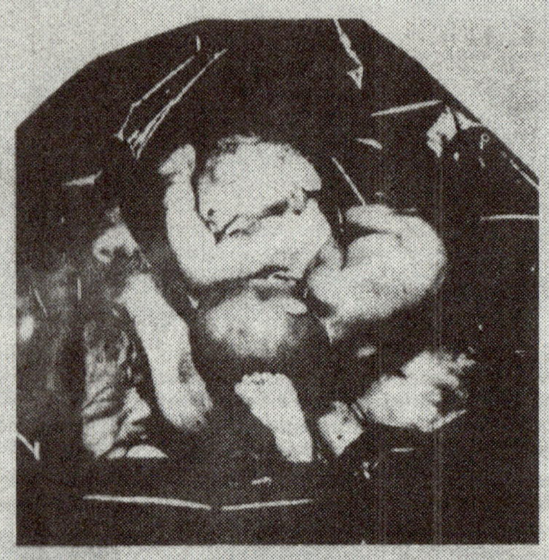

Human Garbage—"These dead babies had reached fetal ages of 18 to 24 weeks before being killed by abortion. This is the result of one morning's work at a Canadian teaching hospital."

(From Handbook on Abortion)

This crime against Creation cannot go unpunished!

Morgentaler's a free man-- Quebec drops all charges

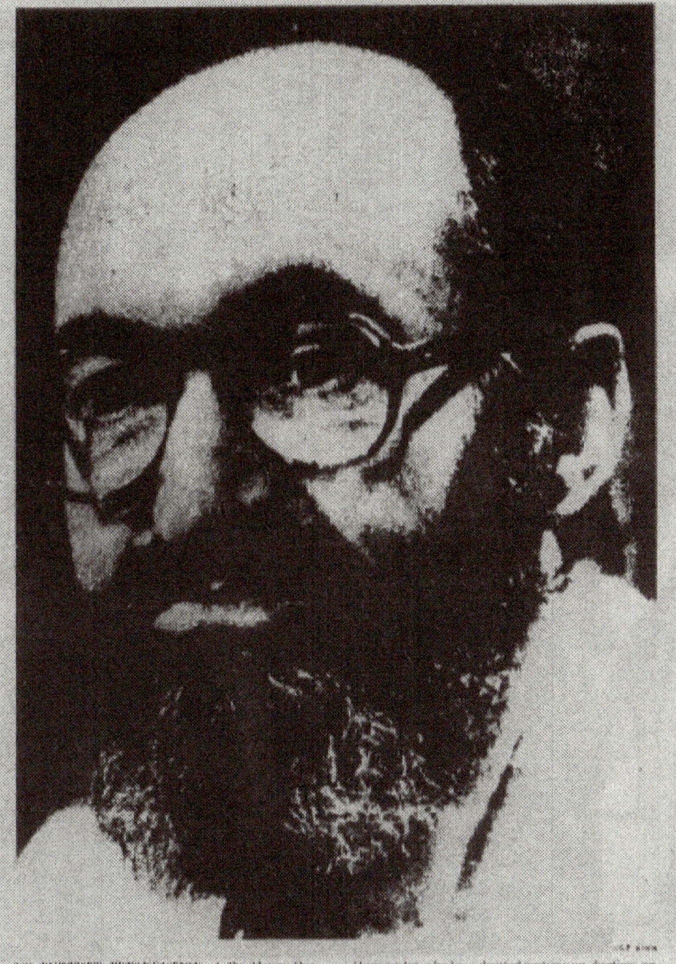

NO FURTHER PROSECUTION of Dr. Henry Morgentaler will be undertaken by the Quebec government. Justice Minister Marc-Andre Bedard announced today. Morgentaler, who has admitted performing abortions on thousands of women in Montreal, has been acquitted three times on charges of performing illegal abortions.

In Hitler's Germany, our Germany, a licence to practice medicine was not a licence for murder. This Jew abortionist would have been removed from our midst and put into a concentration camp where he could no longer claw our young to death in our mothers' wombs.

We loved him because he loved White youth. He treated the young with the love and the respect they deserve as our successors and he made them worthy of that love and respect by training them for responsible adulthood.

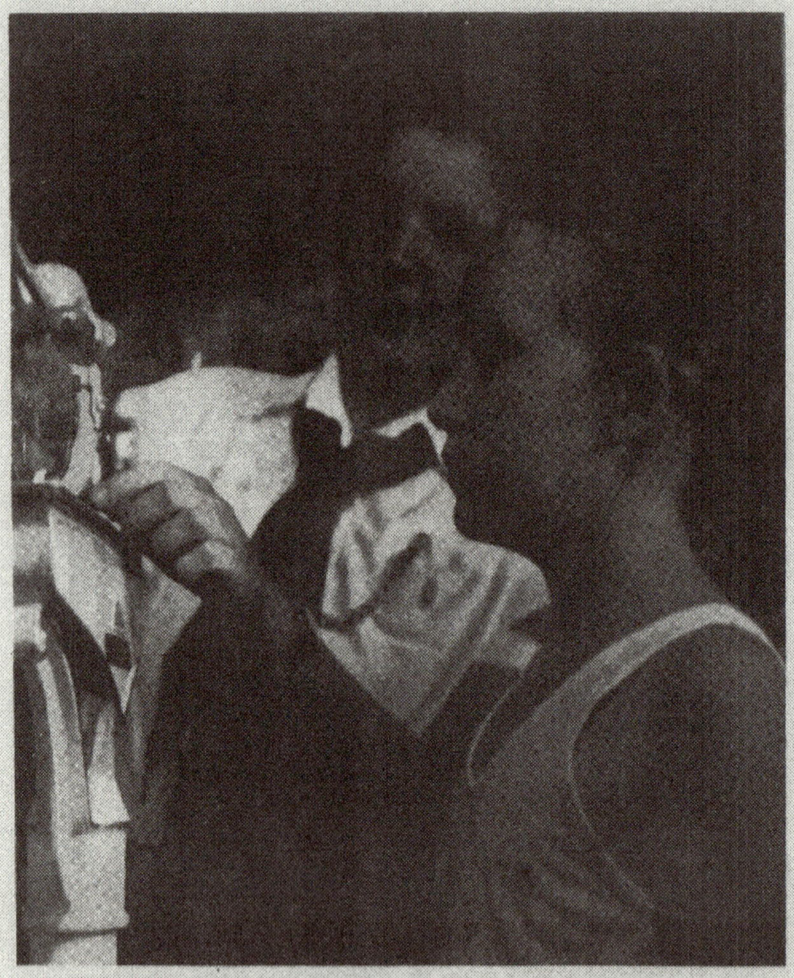

No child was neglected, for how can we neglect those who ensure the continuity of our race?

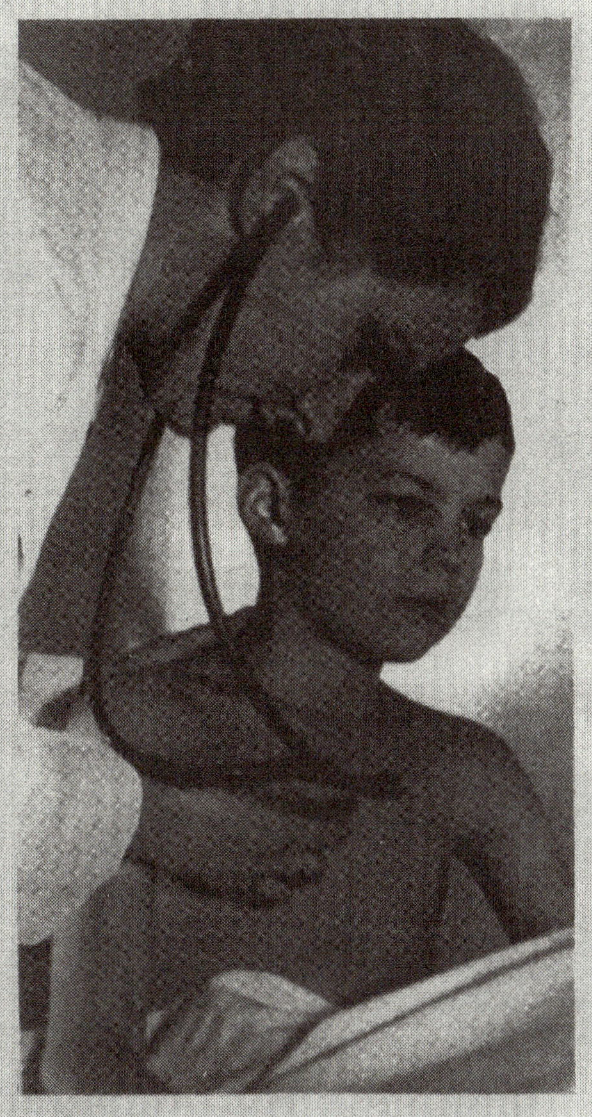

Medical examinations were thorough, regular and compulsory.

We apply Nature's wisdom to the raising of our young. For this, we are called "totalitarians".

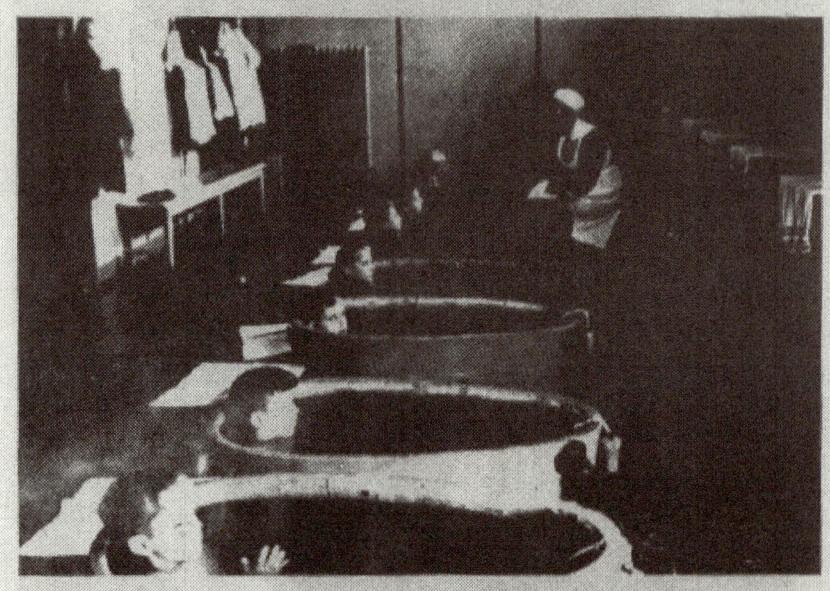

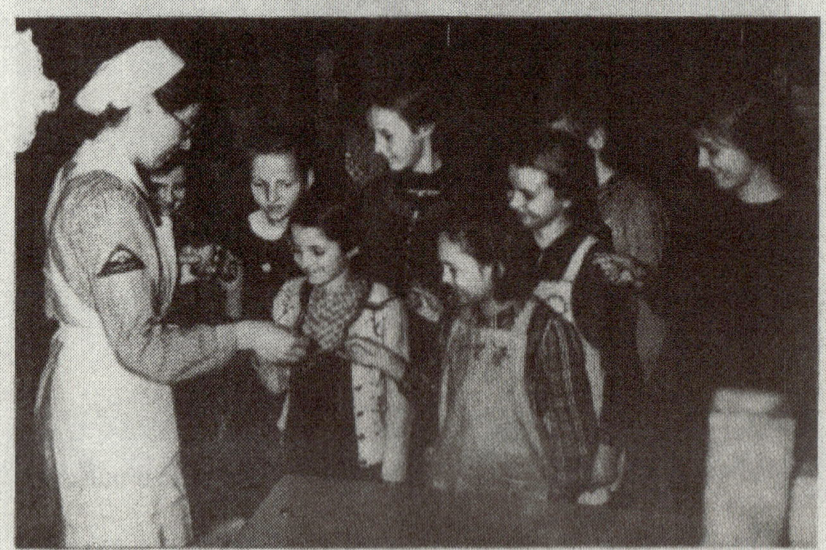

Children receive free vitamin supplements in school.

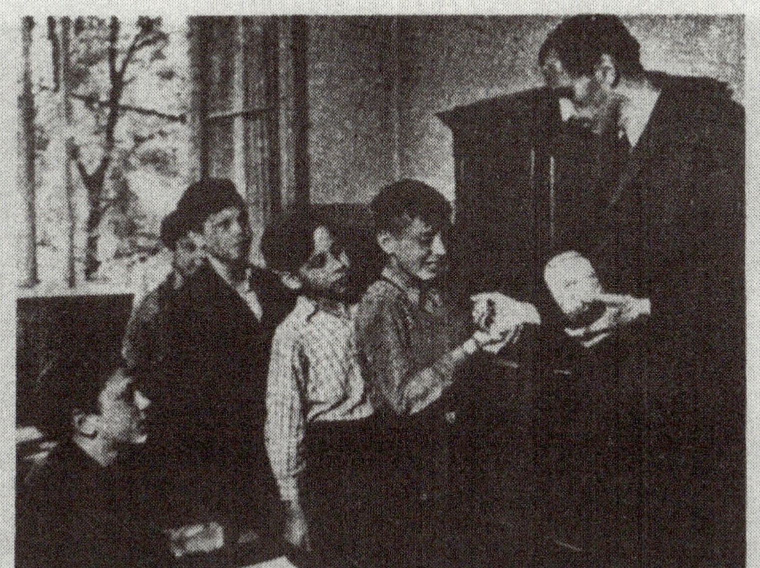

Healthy bodies for healthy minds: Our school-children receive
Vitamin C every day, thanks to Adolf Hitler.

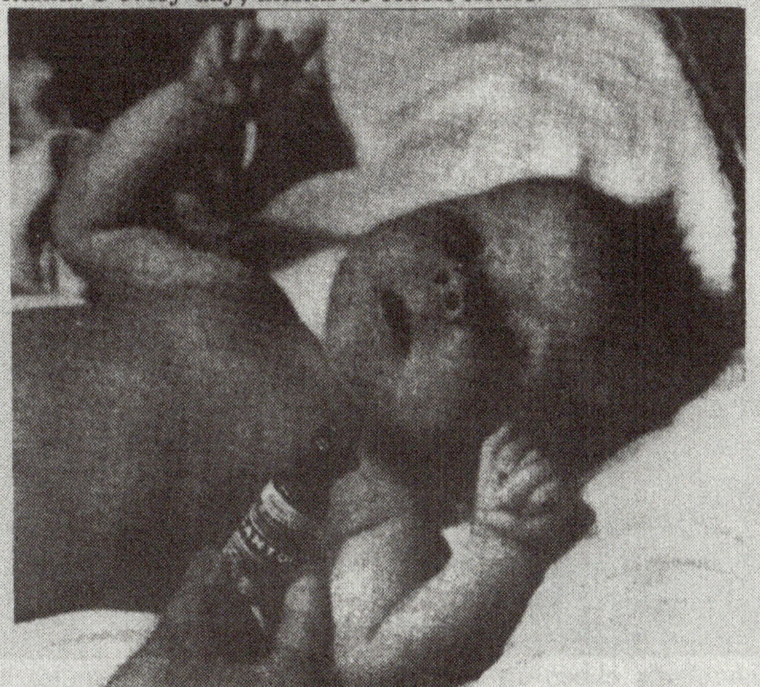

Vitamin D was given to babies to make their bones strong.

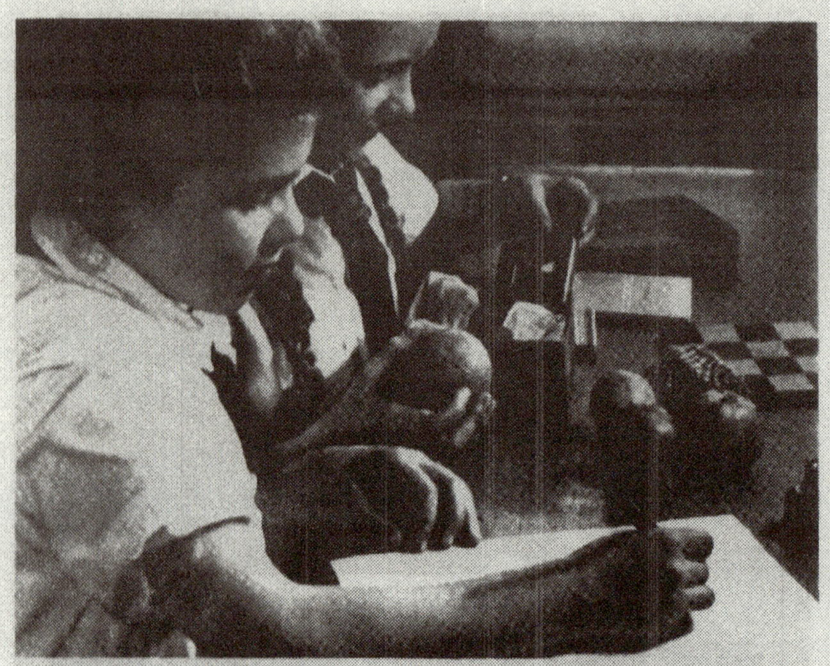

Schoolgirls look forward to their daily fruit.

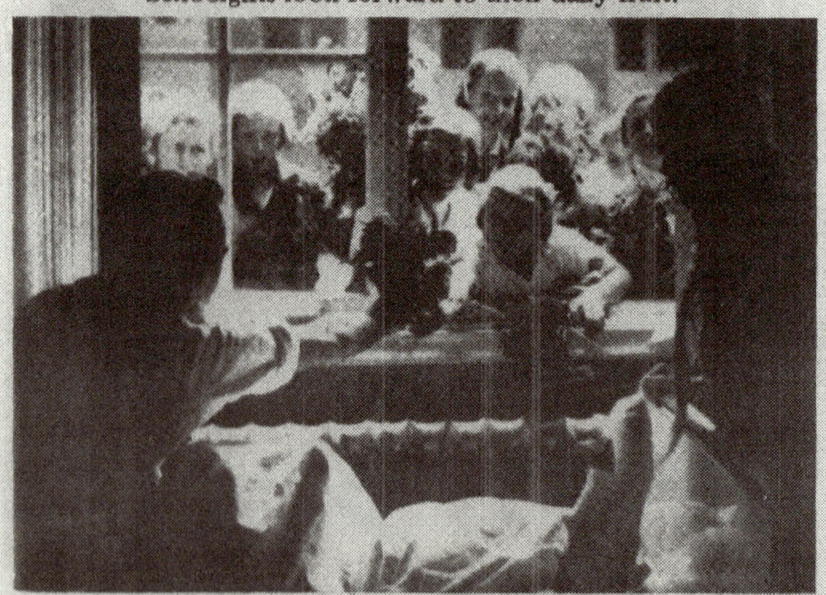

Schoolgirls cheer up our wounded soldiers with smiles and flowers. With children like these, we did not hesitate to sacrifice our lives in their defense.

(translated from the German by Eva-Maria Hood)

In Germany, before Hitler came to power, the colleges were teaching exactly what our colleges are teaching today. One of Hitler's first acts was to fire all the Jew and communists teachers, and replace them with white Christians. The blackboard states:

$$5X5 = 24$$

There are no race problems.
All people are equal.
There are no more nations.
Do away with the mother language.
LEARN - - - - - -EXPERIMENT! !
Kill the seed in the mother's body.
THERE IS NO GOD.
Leave the church.
Disregard father and mother.
Never win a war.
BECOME PACIFISTS.

We loved him because he taught youth the value of hard work, the joy of sport and the appreciation of Nature's outdoors. We learned that we survived and prospered only when we knew our relationship to Nature.

We loved him because he gave our youth hope for the future.

Not only did Adolf Hitler strive mightily to insure the continuity of our race, but also, the continuity of our race's leadership.

Talented youth were selected, regardless of family name or class. Only those who passed the most rigorous examinations were chosen to be candidates for our new leadership schools, the National Political Academies or NAPOLA's.

Instruction was demanding and, at the same time, fulfilling. Healthy minds and healthy bodies demanded the practical as well as the theoretical.

We loved him because he threw off the dead hand of a decaying aristocracy of inbred birth and undeserved privilege, of unearned wealth and class hatred. This he replaced with a new aristocracy of merit: Leaders, not hyphenated figureheads; producers, not conspicuous consumers; creators, not slavish copiers of dubious tradition.

No longer were there "upper" and "lower" classes of youth, but White, European youth!

Hitler was true to himself and to his race. He chose to fight. We loved him for his example of courage, his example of White Manhood.

We loved him because he brought us together, we Europeans.
With him, we knew our strength and felt the awesome
importance of our racial mission, as never before. Yes, he
brought all of us together, even Americans, Russians and
Britons. Willingly, we joined the ranks of his great army and
served the Cause of the White Race. Because we fought to the
end, the end of White Civilization has been avoided. Our
sacrifice was not in vain.

We flocked to defend the Holy Swastika Banner of our race.
White men joined his ranks from all the countries of Europe.

Lithuania   Denmark   Latvia

France

Poland

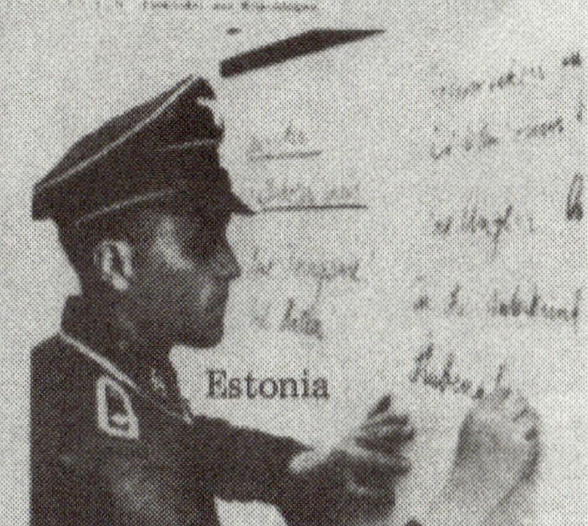
Estonia

America

Norway

Belgium

Spain
Romania
Russia
Bulgaria

We had opened our hearts. Now we opened our pockets to save our race.

Civilians donate metal for the war effort.

We loved him because he honored our heroes. A race without heroes is a dead or dying race. Our White heroes are brave, forthright, strong and kind. Our racial enemy's "heroes" are cowardly, devious, weak and cruel. A race is known by its heroes, because heroes are examples to cherish and to emulate. Thus, do we differ from our enemy, the Jew.

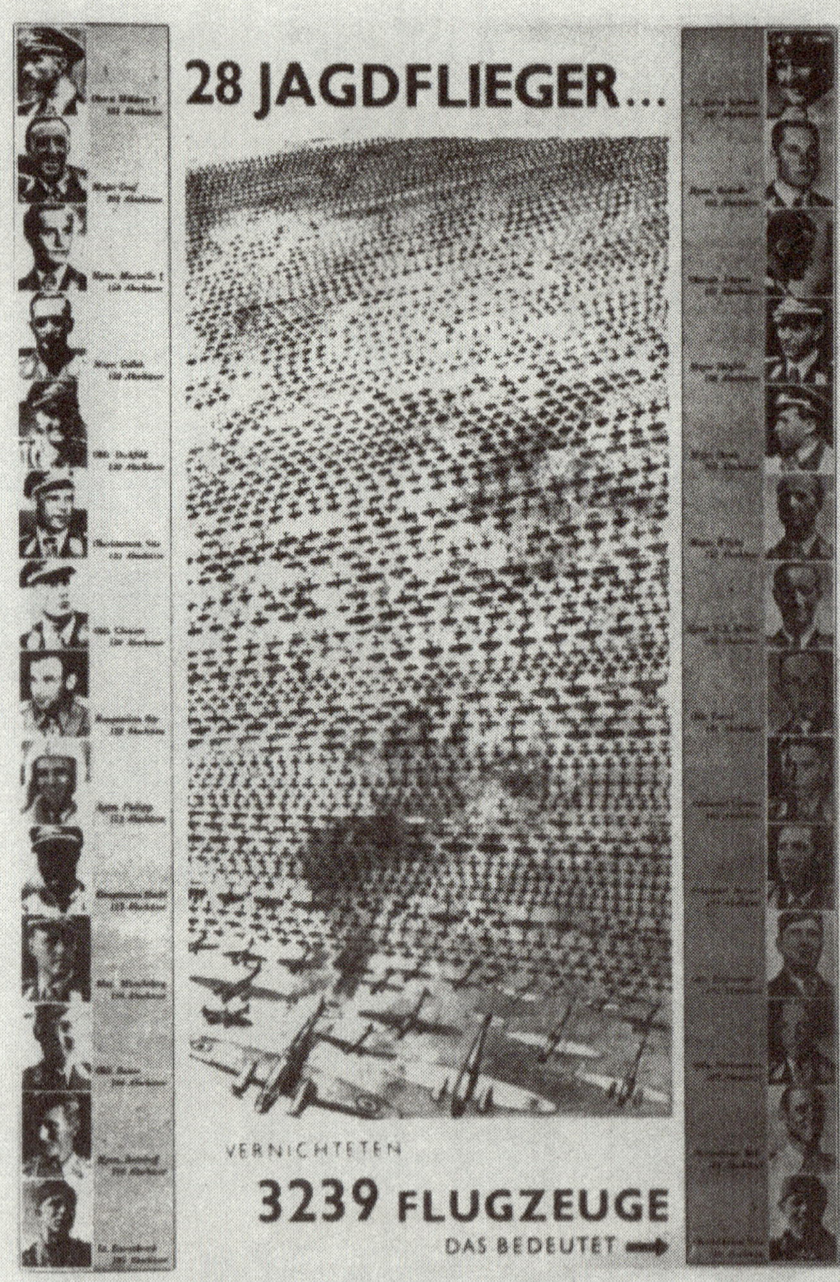

We loved him because he brought out the best in our fighting men. He bestowed upon us a new generation of heroes.

We loved him because he was loyal to our allies and backed his
words with action.

Our Condor Legion, all volunteers, receives the joyous welcome
of the Spaniards they helped to save from Judeo-communism.

We loved him for his greatness in overlooking the mean
propaganda pricks of enemy gadflies.

We loved him for his chivalry, his conduct of war so as to lose as few White lives as possible — friend or foe.

Here, German troops have posted a minefield with clearly-visible warnings in German and English. The White man's object for laying mines was to slow up an enemy advance, not to produce horrible casualties.

We loved him because he was gallant and left our former enemies their pride, even after defeat, in conquered Greece, just as in conquered Dunkirk, Hitler sought only vindication, not annihilation!

We soldiers loved him, for we knew he was right. He knew us, because he was a soldier, too.

We loved him because his spiritual presence prevented our
sufferings and sorrows from overwhelming us.

He was adored like no other mortal, before or since.

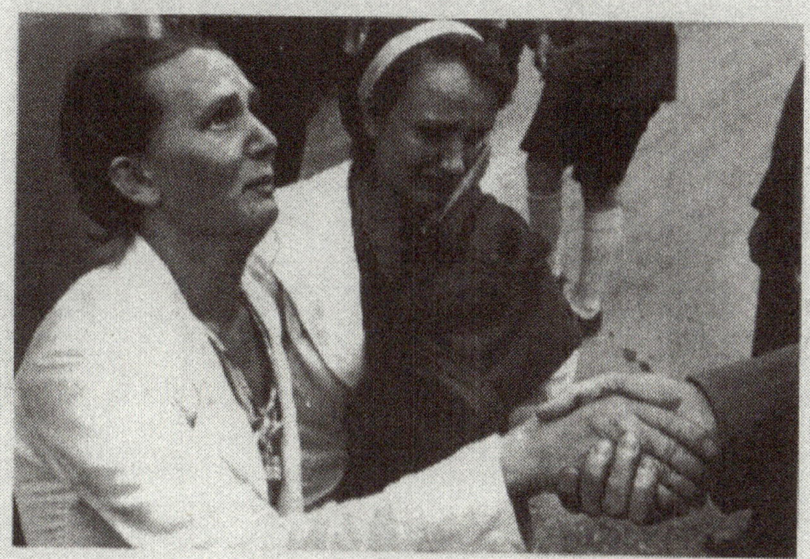

Today, his spirit soars beyond the shores of the White Man's
home in Europe. Wherever we are, he is with us.

WE LOVE YOU, ADOLF HITLER!